Edge Computing and IoT
Scalable Programming Solutions

Table of Contents

Chapter 1. Introduction

Special Report: Edge Computing and IoT: Scalable Programming Solutions

In this engaging and detailed Special Report, we delve into the burgeoning world of edge computing and Internet of Things (IoT), focusing specifically on scalable programming solutions. This expansive subject might seem intimidating due to its technical nature, but don't worry. We have made it our mission to break it down for you, demystify the complexities, and present it all in a digestible and comprehensible manner. Both novices and seasoned tech veterans will explore the transformative potential of edge computing and IoT, discover how they are optimizing operations across various sectors, and learn about the progressive programming solutions that bring scalability and improved performance. Adventure into the advanced technology frontier, fully equipped with insights from our expert analyses, case studies, and industry trends. Let's unlock this knowledge together and give your venture a competitive edge in today's fast-paced digital era.

Chapter 2. Exploring the Fundamentals of Edge Computing and IoT

Edge computing and Internet of Things (IoT) have rapidly emerged as game-changing technologies, transforming the way data processing and communication are conducted across diverse industries. These technologies' concepts, their symbiotic relationship, applications, advantages, and challenges form a critical foundation for comprehending the intricacies of scalable programming solutions.

2.1. Understanding Edge Computing

Edge computing describes a model of computing where data processing happens close to the source of data generation - 'the edge' of the network - rather than in a distant data center or cloud. The intent of edge computing is to minimize latency, reduce bandwidth usage, and enhance the privacy and security of data transmission.

Edge computing is designed around distributed IT architecture, which incorporates local computing and storage solutions. Processing data at the proximity of source devices reduces the need for long-haul data transportations, improving speed, reliability, and efficiency.

In essence, edge computing enables quick real-time data processing with limited connectivity or delay. It's a paradigm shift from the traditional centralized computing models, where data from disparate sources are gathered and processed in a central location.

2.2. Internet of Things (IoT) Explained

IoT encompasses the network of physical objects—'things'—embedded with sensors, software, and other technologies to connect and exchange data with other devices and systems over the internet. These devices could range from simple household items like thermostats and refrigerators to complex industrial tools.

IoT implementation has grown exponentially mainly due to the massive surge in internet usage, decrease in the cost of connected devices, and the acceleration of IPv6 networks.

The key elements of an IoT ecosystem include the physical devices (the 'things'), the communication infrastructure that facilitates data exchange, and the software systems that enable data interpretation for beneficial actions.

2.3. The Intersection of Edge Computing and IoT

While each technology is potent on its own, the true strength lies in their convergence. The alliance of IoT and edge computing has given birth to the possibility of real-time data insights and expedited decision-making processes.

In an IoT scenario, troves of data are constantly generated by 'things', which, without a local processing mechanism, can overwhelm a network. This is where edge computing steps in. It mitigates the challenges posed by extensive data transport by moving the processing job closer to the source of the data.

Hence, edge computing allows for immediate data filtering, analysis, and relay back to the IoT devices in real time. As a result, the tandem of edge computing and IoT can garner actionable insights, render a fast response, and result in improved operational efficiency.

2.4. Benefits of Merging Edge Computing and IoT

The fusion of these two technologies, edge computing and IoT, brings several advantages to system operations.

Firstly, the reduced latency due to localized data processing is crucial for applications needing instant responses, like self-driving cars or cardiac monitors. Processing delays may pose severe threats in these situations.

Secondly, the distributed compute model of edge computing enhances the security and reliability of an IoT network by allowing for more controlled data transmission and reducing the risk of a centralized data breach.

Lastly, edge computing promotes bandwidth efficiency and reduces the cost associated with heavy data transmissions by analyzing and condensing the data at the source itself before it's transported to the cloud for further usage or storage.

2.5. Challenges and Solutions in Implementing Edge Computing and IoT

While the power of the IoT-edge computing combination is undoubtedly promising, it's not without its share of challenges.

The security concerns surrounding these technologies remain

substantial. Edge computing, being distributed, poses risks such as physical tampering and unauthorized access points. On the IoT side, maintaining secure device identity and secure data transit are daunting.

To enact a scalable edge computing and IoT model, a robust security strategy is critical. This strategy should include secure hardware, secure gateways for data transmission, data encryption techniques, and network monitoring systems for real-time threat detection.

Scalability also poses another challenge, given the sheer volume of devices and data involved in the IoT paradigm. However, this can be addressed by incorporating scalable programming solutions that we will delve into in the succeeding sections.

Edge computing and IoT are evolving technologies that will help businesses to be more efficient, responsive, and agile. It's a nuanced blend of data processing, storage and network infrastructure, and intelligent software that harness the power of data produced by the ever-expanding network of IoT devices. Understanding their fundamentals is the first step in harnessing their unsurpassable potential effectively.

Chapter 3. Key Concepts: From Cloud to Edge

The dawn of the technological age brought us the cloud, a critical foundation for businesses in the digital age. Now, we are witnessing the rise of another dramatic shift in computing architecture - Edge Computing.

3.1. Understand the Basics: Cloud and Edge

Cloud computing has been a transcendent technology in recent years, enabling companies to store vast amounts of data and leveraging its computing power anywhere, anytime. The cloud functions by centralizing data storage and computing power in data centers.

On the contrary, edge computing expands this model by moving data processing closer to the source of data, making the processing speedier and more efficient. It essentially relocates the 'intelligence' and power of data processing from a centralized cloud to the 'edge' - i.e., closer to where the data originates.

3.2. The Rationale Behind Edge Computing

Undoubtedly, edge computing wouldn't have become a significant player without the extensive proliferation of IoT devices. The explosion of IoT devices generates an overwhelming amount of data. As the IoT universe expands, it's inevitable that moving all the data to a single central cloud won't be the most efficient solution.

Edge computing addresses this problem by bringing computation and storage facilities closer to source devices. By doing this, it significantly lowers the latency, reduces data transit costs, and ensures real-time data processing, which is crucial for certain IoT applications like self-driving cars traveling at high speeds.

3.3. The Transition: Moving from Cloud to Edge

In reality, while we discuss the shift from cloud to edge, it is not about choosing one over the other. Rather, it's about utilizing the right mix of the two to address the increasing demand for data-driven applications correctly.

Edge doesn't aim to supplant the cloud but to supplement it. It tackles the issues that the cloud cannot address fully, such as latency problems, bandwidth costs, and regulatory compliance concerns over data transportation.

3.4. Edge Computing Components

An edge system comprises mainly of Edge Nodes and Edge Clusters.

1. **Edge Nodes** are physical or virtual devices providing computation and storage services closer to the source of data. They generally include devices like routers, switches, servers, or even an IoT device.

2. **Edge Clusters** are a group of connected edge nodes working in a concert. They provide a higher level of computing power and storage as compared to individual edge nodes.

3.5. Managing Edge Computing Systems

While edge computing presents immense benefits, managing such distributed systems can be challenging. Jobs need to be scheduled accurately across nodes, taking into account the capabilities and resources of each node. Besides, handling edge systems' security and integrating them with cloud systems can be daunting tasks. These complexities necessitate the development of highly scalable programming solutions.

3.6. The Future: A Hybrid Cloud-Edge Ecosystem

The future will witness an astonishing number of connected devices, rapidly increasing the volume of data. To generate valuable insights from this data in real-time, a hybrid cloud-edge computing model will be the ideal solution. As we move forward, the task for businesses and developers will be to create a harmonious balance between the two, leveraging the unique strengths of both cloud and edge computing to establish a truly robust and efficient data model.

In this context, the focus must be on creating scalable programming solutions that can handle vast amounts of data while retaining system stability. The right solutions will not only enable better data processing but also form the bedrock of novel applications and innovations in the IoT landscape, further strengthening the fundamentals of the digital age.

3.7. Conclusion

The journey "from cloud to edge" is not a replacement journey; it's a complementary one. It's about taking the robustness of the cloud and merging it with the immediacy of the edge. The cloud continues to excel as an excellent tool for big data analytics and storage, while the edge bring forth the power of real-time, localized decision making. Together, they form an interconnected system - each building upon the strengths of the other, creating a powerful, efficient, and dynamic landscape for data management, further paving the way for IoT's bright future.

Chapter 4. Diving into the Need for Scalability in Programming Solutions

In the growing world of edge computing and the Internet of Things (IoT), the need for scalability in programming solutions is more compelling than ever before. Developers and tech leaders across industries grapple with enormous amounts of data, fast-changing technology landscapes, and increasing demands for performance. These challenges underscore the indispensability of scalable programming solutions, which promise improved efficiency, cost-effectiveness, and performance enhancement.

4.1. THE DATA DELUGE AND SCALE

Out of the quintillions of bytes of data produced each day, a significant portion is attributed to IoT devices and edge computing processes. The sheer volume, variety, and velocity of this data is beyond the capacity of traditional programming solutions. This huge leap in data production requires scalable programming strategies designed to cope with dynamic data surges and contraction, and efficiently process and manage the data within an acceptable time frame.

Scalable programming solutions form the backbone of modern applications. They can handle growth in data influx, providing a pathway to manage this data in a reliable, timely, and cost-efficient manner. They optimize resources, ensuring that the system's performance does not degrade adversely, despite increasing data loads.

4.2. SCALABILITY AND SYSTEM PERFORMANCE

Scalable solutions not just manage growth, they also improve the overall system performance. They allow data to be processed faster, resulting in reduced latency and improved response times. Edge computing, with its paradigm of processing data close to its source, significantly benefits from this feat.

Programming solutions that scale are designed to squeeze maximal performance from minimal hardware. This is especially vital in edge computing where devices might not boast the most powerful processing capabilities. Scalable programming techniques, therefore, dramatically heighten the potential of edge computing applications, despite the possible hardware constraints.

Further, scalability ensures adequate hardware utilization. Resources are stretched to the fullest potential before additional expense is justified for hardware acquisitions. This results in overall cost savings and optimized compute resource usage.

4.3. DEVELOPMENT AND MAINTENANCE

Scalable programming solutions are not just defined by robustness or elasticity; they also cover easier development and maintenance. Scalability ensures that programmers can easily understand and change the application structure by isolating effects of changes. Coding in scalable languages and platforms allows for effortless scaling up or down.

In addition, it provides a solid basis for the maintenance of the codebase. The ability to easily understand and change aspects of the code affords the opportunity to fix bugs rapider, implement new features seamlessly and ensure a higher quality of the codebase.

4.4. COST-EFFECTIVENESS

Scalability goes hand in hand with cost-effectiveness. It ensures optimal resource utilization, thus resulting in potential cost savings. Through maximizing hardware utility before requiring further investments, and ensuring efficient processing of increased data loads, it dramatically drops the per-unit cost of data processing.

4.5. THE DRAWBACK OF NOT SCALING

The consequences of not implementing scalable programming solutions can be costly. Increased latency, reduced performance, costly overheads, and a system that can't cope with increased demand, all become realities.

The inability of traditional programming techniques to keep pace with growth in data can result in significant bottlenecks. These hinder performance and impact negatively on user experience, both of which can have detrimental consequences for organizations.

4.6. CONCLUSION

In summary, the need for scalability in programming is vital. It ensures high-performing, robust, and cost-effective solutions to manage the data deluge associated with IoT and edge computing. As we continue to generate and rely on larger volumes of data, and as technology continues to advance at an unprecedented rate, the importance of scalable programming solutions will only continue to amplify. Understanding and integrating scalability into your programming engineering practices will set your operations apart, foster innovation, and promote a competitive advantage.

Chapter 5. Architecture and Infrastructure Support for Edge Computing

The architecture and infrastructure for edge computing are vital elements that determine the system's ability to handle, process, and transmit a large stream of data. The characteristics of the ideal architecture are scalability, low latency, bandwidth optimization, and synchronization with the central servers.

5.1. The Physical Architecture of Edge Computing

Edge computing architecture primarily consists of edge devices and edge servers. Edge devices are the IoT devices that directly interact with the environment. These devices capture, transfer, or process data on a smaller scale. On the other hand, edge servers are local servers that handle more significant data processing tasks and serve as an intermediate link between edge devices and the central server.

Edge devices range from small IoT devices like surveillance cameras and smart home appliances to vehicles, drones, and industrial machines. These devices are often constrained by computing power, energy capacities, and network capabilities.

Edge servers or gateways are substantial scale servers that are situated closer to the edge devices. They have superior processing capability compared to edge devices and are apt for executing heavy computational tasks that edge devices cannot handle. They are also responsible for temporarily storing and rapidly transmitting data to the central servers, which is crucial in scenarios where data latency can't afford any delay.

5.2. Communication Infrastructure for Edge Computing

The communication infrastructure is the essential backbone of edge computing architecture. This infrastructure must support high-speed data exchange between edge devices, edge servers, and the central servers. The significant communications technologies used in edge computing are 5G, Wi-Fi, and LPWAN.

5G technology is the game-changer when it comes to edge computing. It offers greater bandwidth and incredibly low latency, which opens up possibilities for real-time data analysis and decision-making at the edge. This technology also enables remote device management, delivering a massive growth factor for IoT and edge computing.

Wi-Fi remains a robust local area communication medium. With the advent of Wi-Fi 6 and its improvements in terms of capacity, performance, and latency, Wi-Fi plays a crucial role in indoor IoT applications where interference is high.

Low Power Wide Area Network (LPWAN) is a wireless telecommunication technology designed to support long-range communications with a low bit rate. LPWAN technologies are perfect for applications where end devices are scattered across vast distances, such as smart city applications or large-scale agricultural IoT systems.

5.3. Edge Computing Infrastructure Software

Software plays an equally significant role in edge computing alongside hardware. Edge computing infrastructure software comprises the operating system, storage system, cloud-based services, and application software.

The most common choices for the operating system in edge computing infrastructure involve Linux or a real-time operating system (RTOS). Both are open-source technologies with extensive support. RTOS is best suited for time-sensitive IoT applications, where it's vital to have a real-time response.

The role of the storage system in edge computing is to manage the high-volume data generated by IoT devices. These systems need to swiftly store, retrieve, and organize this data stream. Many edge devices apply cloud-based storage systems, offering scalability and high-speed access.

Cloud services play a foundational role in edge computing, providing the backbone that supports infinite scalability, powerful computing power, and storage facilities. Cloud-based services such as AWS Lambda and Azure IoT Edge offer high-level and scalable computing resources to edge devices.

The application software is the ultimate fulcrum that decides the functionality of the edge devices. This software interprets and processes digital signals from sensors, performs decision-making tasks, and interacts with other devices and servers.

5.4. Security Infrastructure for Edge Computing

Highly distributed edge infrastructure presents unique security challenges. Edge devices, due to their sheer numbers and often lacking in-built security, become potential points of vulnerability. The edge computing infrastructure needs to incorporate a dynamic security protocol, including data integrity checks, encryption techniques, intrusion detection, and rapid response to potential breaches.

With a comprehensive and robust architecture, edge computing promises optimum utilization of resources. This efficiency reduces the latency associated with data transmission and processing, paving the way for real-time data-driven applications powering the world's digital transformation.

Chapter 6. The Intersection of IoT and Edge Computing: Advantages and Challenges

Edge computing and the Internet of Things (IoT) are two technological trends that have grown increasingly intertwined. Each presents a unique set of advantages and challenges, which are only amplified when these fields intersect. From this intersection, a new era of highly distributed, data-rich, and dynamic applications is emerging.

6.1. What is Edge Computing and IoT

Edge computing is a distributed computing paradigm aimed at bringing computation and data storage closer to the source of data generation. Contrarily, IoT is about connecting physical devices to the internet, granting them the ability to collect and share data. Together, these technologies allow for the analysis and application of data in real-time, a crucial characteristic for many industries and applications.

6.2. The Advantages of IoT and Edge Computing Intersection

The integration of IoT with edge computing offers numerous benefits. Firstly, it addresses the issue of latency in IoT networks. By processing data at the edge of the network, reactions to real-time conditions can be made faster. This capability is vital in applications such as autonomous vehicles, factory automation, and telemedicine, where split-second decisions can make a difference.

Secondly, this intersection aids in data volume and management. Edge computing can process data locally, reducing the bandwidth needed for data transfer and subsequently leading to cost reductions and efficiency improvement in network usage.

Lastly, edge computing can improve the privacy and security of IoT devices. By keeping data processing closer to the source, the exposure of sensitive information to potential threats during transmission is limited.

6.3. The Challenges in the Intersection of IoT and Edge Computing

Despite the advantages, the convergence of IoT and edge computing presents several challenges. The primary challenge is the complexity in implementing edge computing in existing IoT infrastructures. Embedding intelligence in various edge devices necessitates an understanding of diverse device capabilities, networking services, and data policies.

The second challenge revolves around security and privacy. Although edge computing reduces the risk of data exposure during transmission, the high distribution of data and computation increases the surface area for potential attacks.

The third challenge is about management and orchestration. In an edge environment, applications and resources should be managed across many diverse and geographically distributed sites. Given the sheer scale of devices and data involved in IoT applications, efficient orchestration becomes quite challenging.

6.4. Edge Computing and IoT: Case Studies

Several sectors have begun leveraging the integration of edge computing and IoT to deliver innovative solutions.

In the healthcare industry, edge computing allows real-time processing of patient data collected through various IoT devices. This setup helps in quick detection of any anomalies, thereby enabling immediate action in emergencies.

The retail industry uses edge computing combined with IoT for inventory management. IoT sensors track products and provide real-time stock updates. At the same time, edge computing enables processing this data on-site in each store, reducing the demand for central processing resources and enhancing responsiveness.

Despite the profound potential, the integration of edge computing with IoT is in its early stages. Thus, there's a need for functional programming solutions that can help overcome the deployment challenges and enable the broader adoption and scalability of these technologies.

6.5. Scalable Programming Solutions for IoT and Edge Computing

Scalable programming solutions can help overcome some of the challenges associated with the intersection of IoT and edge computing.

One approach can be to adopt distributed data processing systems like Apache Flink, which provides low-latency, scalable, and resilient stream processing. The critical advantage of this system is that it can run effectively on IoT devices and at the edge, as well as in the cloud.

New programming models and frameworks, such as Eclipse ioFog, are being developed to cater to the specific needs of edge computing in IoT setups. ioFog provides a decentralised platform that allows deployment, orchestration, and security management at the edges of the network.

Adoption of programming solutions that support data partitioning can also be beneficial. It allows the splitting of an extensive dataset across several smaller edge nodes, reducing the processing load on each device and thereby improving overall system performance.

6.6. The Future of IoT and Edge Computing

The intersection of IoT and edge computing is forging the future of numerous industries, enabling dynamic, real-time, and innovative applications. Strong investments are being made and will continue to be made in this space as more industries see the potential for operational optimisation, cost efficiency, and improved customer experiences.

However, to fully exploit the capabilities of these technologies, businesses need to approach the challenges strategically. The development of scalable and efficient programming solutions, standards and practices for security, and efficient management frameworks will facilitate the seamless integration of IoT devices with edge computing infrastructure, enabling a new era of data-rich and powerful applications.

Chapter 7. Data Management and Security in Edge computing

Edge computing extends data processing to the edges of the network, closer to the sources of data. This paradigm shift presents novel opportunities but also brings with it very real challenges in data management and security. In this chapter, we delve into the problems associated with data storage, manipulation, transmission, and security within the edge computing ecosystem.

7.1. Understanding the Data Management Challenge

Edge computing involves a wide range of interconnected devices spread across different geographical locations, with each device having unique storage constraints. Achieving uniform and efficient data management in such a heterogeneous network is a formidable task. One key challenge is balancing the trade-off between local device storage and network latency introduced when sending data to the cloud. An effective data management strategy must minimize latency, maximize device usage, and ensure the consistency and availability of data.

7.2. Exploring Solutions for Storage and Data Manipulation

Several approaches can address storage constraints and facilitate efficient data manipulation in edge computing. One solution is the use of Data Federation, where various devices act together as a virtual system, providing an aggregated view of global data. This system relies on powerful middleware to translate and orchestrate the operations between different data formats and models.

Another emerging approach is edge data life-cycle management, which aims to manipulate data at the edge in a manner similar to centralized cloud data centers. This approach considers the full life-cycle of data —from creation, processing, storage, usage, and ultimately deletion— adopted to the edge computing environment.

7.3. The Role of Distributed Databases

Distributed databases play a crucial role in achieving a unified, shared data layer across geographically dispersed edge nodes. They deliver high availability and fault tolerance, even with network partitions. While distributed databases vary in their structure and operability, a common feature is data replication, where data is copied across numerous nodes to maintain consistent data state. They employ various consistency models and conflict resolution techniques, from eventual consistency, strict consistency to causal consistency.

7.4. Ensuring Data Transmission Security

Security is a significant factor in managing data transmissions due to the vulnerability of edge devices to attacks. The implementation of secure communication protocols and encryption techniques can mitigate these risks. In addition, use of techniques like Mutual Authentication, where both client and servers certify each other before initiating a communication, can significantly improve the security of data exchange.

7.5. Data Privacy and Confidentiality

Data privacy in edge computing environments is yet another significant concern. Here, measures like anonymization, pseudononymization, and secure multi-party computation come into play. Anonymization techniques render personal data unidentifiable, eliminating the possibility of associating data with particular individuals. Pseudonymization, on the other hand, replaces identifiable fields within the data with artificial identifiers.

Secure Multi-party Computation (SMPC) is a cryptographic technique that allows multiple parties to cooperate in the computation of a function over their inputs while keeping those inputs private.

7.6. Concluding remarks

Data management and security in edge computing brings about unique challenges. However, innovative approaches for storage and manipulation, together with robust security measures, can address these issues effectively. As technology evolves, further research and new strategies will be continuously developed to tackle these challenges. Edge computing opens a wide realm of opportunities, and with effective data management and security protocols, we can harness its full potential.

Chapter 8. Demystifying Scalable Programming Languages for Edge and IoT

Scalable programming languages have the ability to handle growing amounts of work by either adding resources to the system or making use of the existing ones in a better way. This capability is essential in the context of edge computing and IoT, where devices often need to perform tasks promptly and efficiently, dealing with large-scale networks and high-volume data processing.

Understanding the internals of these languages and how they can be used to leverage the benefits of IoT and edge computing can seem intimidating. However, a systematic approach can make this task more manageable.

8.1. Key Characteristics of Scalable Languages

There are certain essential characteristics that a programming language should have to ensure scalability, especially in the IoT context. Let's explore them side-by-side.

- **Concurrent Execution:** This allows a language to execute or carry out multiple computations or processes simultaneously. This is especially important in the IoT sphere, where several tasks often need to be executed at once.

- **Efficient Memory Management:** This helps reduce the risk of system crashes and enhances application performance. Given the limited resources in edge devices, this becomes even more critical.

- **Event Handling:** Since IoT is driven largely by the concept of 'events' (like sensor readings), a language must be good at managing these events.

- **Fault Tolerance & Resilience:** IoT networks, given their complexity and distributed nature, are susceptible to faults. A scalable language must be able to handle faults gracefully.

- **Support for Real-Time Processing:** Many applications, especially those at the edge, require real-time data processing capabilities, which a scalable programming language should provide.

With these characteristics outlined, let's dive into some of the languages that meet these criteria.

8.2. JavaScript/Node.js for Edge and IoT

JavaScript, when used with Node.js runtime, is a popular choice for developing IoT applications at the edge due to its asynchronous, event-driven nature, which can handle multiple tasks concurrently.

Node.js utilizes a single-threaded event loop architecture to handle multiple concurrent clients efficiently- an ideal situation for real-time IoT applications. Its light memory footprint, coupled with non-blocking I/O (input/output), ensures efficient performance even on resource-constrained edge devices.

Moreover, being one of the most popular languages globally, JavaScript benefits from a large, supportive community and an abundance of open-source libraries and tools, which further simplifies IoT application development and reduces time-to-market.

8.3. Python for Edge and IoT

Python is another widely-used language in the IoT space due to its simplicity, readability, and extensive library support, offering modules like NumPy and SciPy for numerical computation, and libraries such as pandas for data manipulation.

This interpreted high-level language has built-in support for memory management, which is advantageous in handling complex applications with less risk of crashes. However, it's important to note that, in contrast to languages like Node.js, Python is not natively built for concurrent execution, although libraries like asyncio can provide some concurrency capabilities.

Due to its ease of learning and use, Python can be an excellent choice for developing quick IoT prototypes. However, for heavy real-time and concurrent processing at the edge, other languages might be more appropriate.

8.4. Go for Edge and IoT

The Go language, designed at Google, has gained popularity for its simplicity and performance. It has built-in support for concurrent programming, making it an excellent candidate for high-performance edge and IoT applications.

Go has efficient garbage collection mechanisms, provides robust error handling, and is compiled to machine code, thus offering faster execution times - a crucial factor for real-time edge computing applications. The language also includes a rich standard library and is statically typed, which can help prevent many runtime errors.

A notable downside, however, is that Go isn't as widely adopted as JavaScript or Python, which could mean fewer community resources and libraries.

8.5. Rust for Edge and IoT

Rust is a systems programming language that prioritizes speed, memory safety, and parallelism. It's known for its ability to manage memory without the need for a garbage collector, which can be a crucial benefit for low-resource environments in edge computing and IoT devices.

Moreover, Rust's support for concurrent programming and its strong type system, aiding in catching errors at compile time, make it an attractive option for complex, high-performing edge computing applications.

However, Rust's steep learning curve might deter many developers. It's also less mature and has fewer libraries compared to languages like JavaScript and Python.

Each of these programming languages brings unique advantages within the context of edge computing and IoT, reflecting different trade-offs between flexibility, performance, safety, and learning curve. It's essential to choose the right language based on the specific requirements and constraints of a given IoT or edge computing project.

Emerging technologies like WebAssembly (Wasm) are also showing great promise in edge computing, due to their ability to run code closely to native speed while maintaining a sandboxed environment.

As edge computing and IoT continue to evolve, so does the need for innovative and scalable programming solutions. The path toward such solutions lies not just in choosing the right programming languages, but also in how we design, implement, and optimize our applications to make the most of the resources at hand.

Chapter 9. Real-world Use Cases and Applications

Today's digital world operates in real-time, and edge computing, coupled with IoT, offers an impressive framework to meet this demand. It is not enough to be aware of these technologies - their practical implementation and the value they add to various sectors is critical to understand. Let us delve into some real-world applications and use cases to better comprehend the impact of edge computing and IoT.

9.1. Industrial Automation

Edge computing and IoT have revolutionized the industrial sector, including manufacturing, logistics, and supply chains. In factories, IoT devices gather real-time data from machines, while edge computing allows for immediate analysis and response. This combination reduces downtime, prevents catastrophic failures, and enhances operational efficiency.

Consider an automotive manufacturing plant as an example. IoT sensors embedded in machines monitor performance, predict imminent malfunctions, and alert operators. Edge computing systems then process this vast amount of data on-site, facilitating quick decision making and maintaining continuous production.

9.2. Smart Cities

With a growing global urban population, cities are turning to edge computing and IoT to enhance the quality of life and create safer, more efficient urban environments. From traffic management to public safety, waste disposal to smart buildings, these technologies are shaping future cities.

Imagine a scenario where an IoT-enabled traffic management system collects real-time data from road sensors, cameras, and citizen reports. An edge computing system analyzes this data, adjusting traffic signals in real-time to relieve congestion and improve flow. Additionally, information on traffic jams, accidents, and optimal routes can be communicated instantly to drivers and authorities, facilitating efficient urban mobility.

9.3. Healthcare

In healthcare, edge computing and IoT can transform patient care and outcomes. Sensors can collect critical health data from patients, such as heart rate or glucose levels, and transmit this information to edge computing devices for immediate analysis. This enables real-time monitoring and mitigates life-threatening emergencies by alerting medical teams to sudden changes in patient conditions.

For example, consider a wearable device like a smartwatch that monitors a diabetic person's blood sugar levels in real-time. With edge computing, this real-time data can be analyzed, and if a dangerous trend is detected, an alert can be sent to the individual and their healthcare provider enabling immediate action and possibly prevent a medical crisis.

9.4. Retail

In the retail sector, edge computing and IoT are enhancing the customer experience and streamlining operations. Smart shelves fitted with weight sensors can detect when stock is low and automatically update inventory systems, while customer data can be analyzed at the edge to deliver personalized shopping experiences.

Imagine a supermarket where IoT sensors and cameras monitor and analyze customer behaviors—such as time spent in a specific aisle or purchases made. An edge computing system processes this data in real-time, providing the retailer with immediate insights to optimize store layouts, product placements, or personalized promotions, thus boosting sales.

9.5. Agriculture

In agriculture, edge computing and IoT enable precision farming, which increases productivity and sustainability. IoT devices collect data about soil moisture, crop health, and weather conditions, while edge computing systems analyze this data locally, enabling farmers to make more informed decisions about irrigation, fertilization, and pest control.

Consider an apple orchard employing IoT sensors to measure soil humidity, sunlight, and temperature. With edge computing, these measurements could be processed on-site and a predictive model for optimal watering and fertilization schedules developed, maximizing the harvest while minimizing resource use.

On a comprehensive note, the blend of edge computing and IoT is opening a myriad of opportunities in various sectors by enabling real-time analysis and decision-making. This is just the tip of the iceberg - with more innovation and integration, the scope is endless. It is clear that understanding and investing in these technologies will be critical for remaining competitive in a rapidly evolving digital landscape. Now that we have familiarized ourselves with real-world applications and use cases, in the next section, we will further examine the scalable programming solutions that enable these technologies and how they can be effectively implemented for maximum benefit.

Chapter 10. Future Trends and Predictions in Edge Computing and IoT

As the digital landscape moves toward decentralization, edge computing and IoT continue to evolve at a remarkable rate. Growth seldom comes without birthing new trends and directions. Let's dive into these forthcoming trajectories that could potentially shape the future of edge computing and Internet of Things.

10.1. Emerging IoT applications in Edge Computing

IoT devices are continuing to expand across sectors such as healthcare, infrastructure, retail, transportation, and more. Each of these sectors is realizing the possibilities and potential that IoT devices can bring when connected with edge computing. The health sector, for example, is exploring IoT for remote patient monitoring, leveraging edge computing to analyze and respond to data in real-time. Similarly, the transport sector is embracing IoT for vehicle tracking, routing and diagnostics, wherein edge computing enables faster processing and decision-making.

In the retail sector, IoT and edge computing are being employed for inventory management and customer behaviour analysis. With edge devices analysing IoT data on-site, retailers can dynamically adapt their strategies based on real-time consumer behaviour and stock levels.

10.2. Rise of Autonomous Things

Autonomous systems like self-driving cars, drones, robots, and automated appliances are increasing in prevalence. These systems thrive on real-time analysis and decision-making, making them prime instances of edge computing. As machine learning algorithms become more sophisticated, we can expect to see Autonomous Things (AuT) increasingly incorporate edge computing to reduce latency, relieve network congestion, and enhance performance.

Drones, for instance, are fantastic examples of AuT that possess the immense potential for edge applications. They operate in environments that can be remote and inaccessible. Such circumstances necessitate offline functioning and quick decision-making capabilities, which are facilitated by edge computing.

10.3. Data Security and Privacy

As edge computing tends to process data at the source, it can significantly mitigate the risks of data breaches and cyber attacks. However, the interconnectedness among IoT devices opens new threats to privacy and security. Degrees of vulnerability to cyber attacks vary due to the heterogeneous nature of IoT devices. Consequently, future developments must prioritize robust security protocols and measures.

As edge IoT devices collect and process sensitive data in real time, they need to adopt advanced encryption and secure access management to prevent unauthorized access. The development of security-oriented hardware for edge devices is another potential trend.

10.4. Energy Efficiency

Energy efficiency is a trending concern in both edge computing and IoT. IoT devices are often battery-powered or use energy harvesting techniques to function. As the number of these devices grows exponentially, so does the overall energy consumption. Edge computing can address this dilemma by processing data on-site and decreasing the number of data transmitted over networks, hence reducing energy consumption.

Research is also underway to harness eco-friendly, sustainable sources of energy for powering IoT devices, such as solar or wind energy. The more IoT devices can operate on renewable energy sources, the more sustainable and 'greener' the IoT-Edge ecosystem will become.

10.5. Interoperability and Standardization

The vast diversity of IoT devices poses challenges for interoperability and standardization. The current lack of unified standards results in proprietary IoT solutions, potentially leading to issues with communication and compatibility between devices.

Standardization bodies are working on developing unified standards to address this problem. The Open Connectivity Foundation (OCF), the Thread Group, and the Industrial Internet Consortium (IIC) are just a few of the organizations pushing for IoT standards that can ensure compatibility and interoperability in the edge-IoT ecosystem.

In conclusion, as edge computing and IoT technology continue to evolve, it paves the way for the new trends and prospects mentioned above. Coupled with advances in machine learning and artificial intelligence, these technologies hold the promise to reshape the way we live and work in the future profoundly. We can expect significant ripple effects across many sectors, and those who adapt most effectively to these changes will enjoy a considerable competitive edge. The challenge for all stakeholders, from developers to users, will be to keep pace with this evolution, embracing changes while addressing the associated challenges. Only then we can fully unlock the enormous potential of this exciting frontier.

Chapter 11. Designing Your Own Scalable Solution: A Practical guide

Creating a scalable IoT solution hinges on a couple of key technical considerations and design choices. Implementing a flexible and scalable system architecture, coupled with a rigorous approach to programming, will be instrumental for success.

11.1. Understanding the Basics of Scalability

To start, scalability is the ability of a system, network, or process to handle a growing amount of work or its potential to be enlarged to accommodate that growth. Scalable solutions need to accommodate more devices, data, and users as the demands increase over time. In the IoT and edge computing paradigm, this means your systems must manage an increasing number of connected devices efficiently without compromising the performance or functionality of your solution.

Scalability can be classified into two types: vertical and horizontal. Vertical scaling, often termed "scaling up", involves adding resources such as memory, processing power, or storage to a single node in the system, typically a server. Despite its simplicity, vertical scaling has its limits due to the physical constraints inherent in available technology.

Horizontal scaling, or "scaling out", involves adding more nodes to the system, allowing it to handle more tasks concurrently and distribute the load among multiple resources. This variant of scaling is consistent with the principles of edge computing, where computing resources are distributed closer to the origin of data.

11.2. Designing Scalable Architectures

The key to an effective and scalable IoT solution is in the design of the architecture, which largely dictates the capabilities of the system with respect to how it handles growing workloads. A well-designed architecture should be divided into modules that can work independently but interact effectively with other components.

A modular design promotes scalability by allowing individual components or subsystems to be upgraded without disrupting the operation of the system as a whole. If a module needs to handle a larger workload, it can be equipped with additional resources (vertical scaling) or replicated across multiple instances (horizontal scaling) depending on the design.

When designing your architecture, consider these crucial factors:

- IoT devices: Devices should be as simple as possible to lower costs and enhance ease of deployment. Whenever possible, devices should perform minimal processing and defer heavy workloads to edge servers.

- Communication: The protocol should be light-weighted to cater to devices with constrained resources. MQTT or CoAP can be considered based on your requirements.

- Edge computing: Use edge servers to process data locally, reducing latency and load on cloud servers. Make sure the edge servers are robustly designed, with a focus on capacity and responsiveness.

- Cloud interaction: Cloud servers should only be involved in tasks that require heavy processing or long-term data storage. They must be ready to handle bulk data loads from multiple edge servers simultaneously.

11.3. Choosing the Right Programming Approach

The choice of programming languages, tools, and techniques has a direct impact on the scalability of your solution. You need to consider your project requirements and constraints, as well as familiarity and proficiency in certain languages and environments. Opt for languages with strong community support, extensive libraries, and efficient development tools, such as Python or Java.

Language choice aside, there are several software development strategies you can employ to promote scalability:

- Event-driven programming: Since IoT and edge computing infrastructure often deal with a plethora of events or signals from devices or servers, adopting an event-driven strategy can be beneficial. It allows your software to respond rapidly to simultaneous or asynchronous events.

- Concurrency and parallel processing: Opt for languages or frameworks that support concurrent execution and parallel processing to handle multiple tasks simultaneously and make the most of your available resources.

- Microservices: Instead of a monolithic design, go for a microservices architecture. This approach allows the system to handle tasks independently and scale when necessary, without affecting other subsystems.

11.4. Bringing it all together

Designing and implementing a scalable solution incorporating Edge computing and IoT is not an easy task, but thoughtful design, smart architectural decisions, and an efficient programming approach can streamline the process. By understanding the concepts and strategies cited above, you should be well on your way to building a solution that scales well with growth, whether in terms of devices managed, data processed, or users serviced.

Remember to rigorously test your system and introduce artificial loads to see how it performs under strained conditions. Don't forget to monitor resources and make adjustments as necessary.

Let your vision of the future load guide your decisions today as you build your scalable IoT and edge computing system. Good luck in your journey towards shaping a more responsive and versatile digital infrastructure!